CHRISTMAS CAROLS for Mandolin

CONTENTS

Arranged by Jim Schustedt

ISBN 13: 978-1-4234-1398-9

7777 W. BLUEMOUND RD. P.O. BOX 13819 MILWAUKEE, WI 53213

In Australia contact:
Hal Leonard Australia Pty. Ltd.
4 Lentara Court
Cheltenham, Victoria, 3192 Australia
Email: ausadmin@halleonard.com

Visit Hal Leonard Online at
www.halleonard.com

Angels We Have Heard on High

Traditional French Carol
Translated by James Chadwick

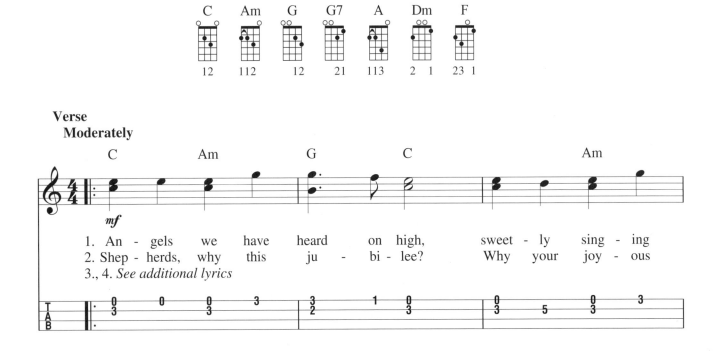

Verse
Moderately

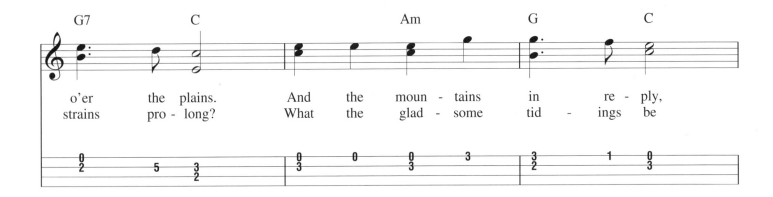

1. An - gels we have heard on high, sweet - ly sing - ing
2. Shep - herds, why this ju - bi - lee? Why your joy - ous
3., 4. *See additional lyrics*

o'er the plains. And the moun - tains in re - ply,
strains pro - long? What the glad - some tid - ings be

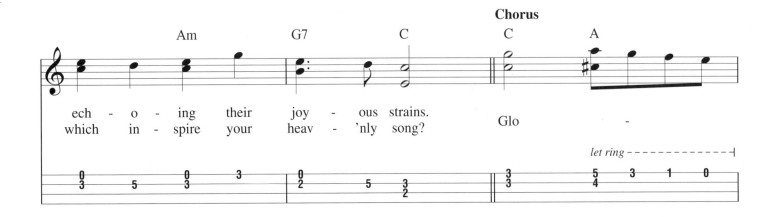

ech - o - ing their joy - ous strains.
which in - spire your heav - 'nly song?

Glo -

let ring

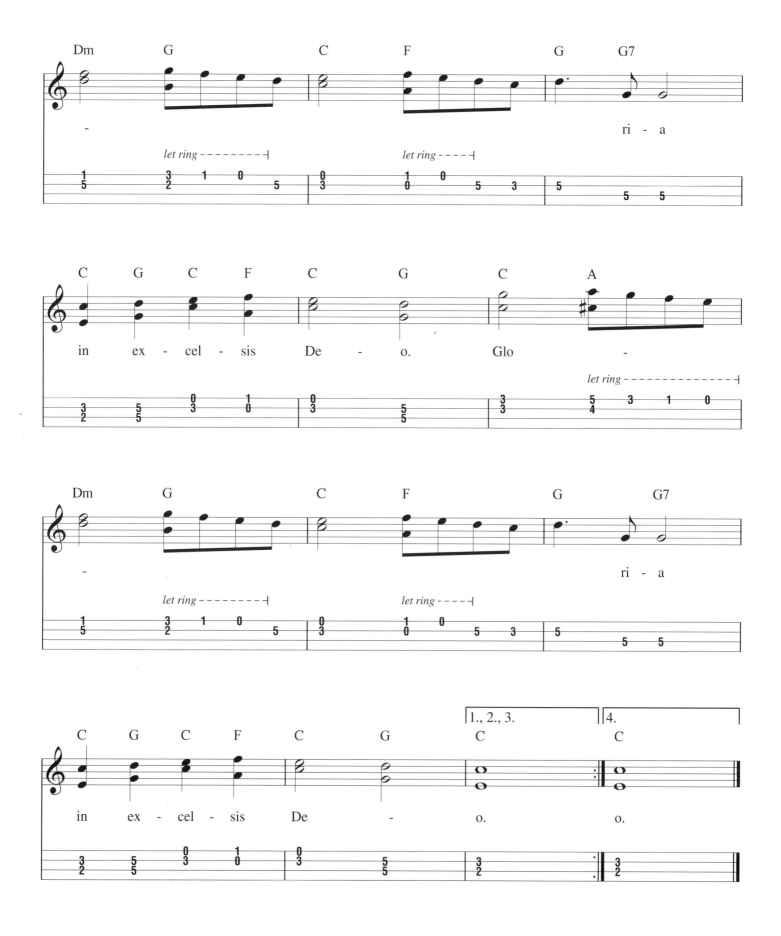

Additional Lyrics

3. Come to Bethlehem and see
   Him whose birth the angels sing;
   Come, adore on bended knee
   Christ the Lord, the newborn King.

4. See within a manger laid
   Jesus, Lord of heaven and earth!
   Mary, Joseph, lend your aid,
   With us sing our Savior's birth.

Away in a Manger

Traditional
Words by John T. McFarland (v.3)
Music by James R. Murray

D   G   A   A7   Em

Verse

Sweetly

1. A - way in a man - ger, no crib for a
2., 3. *See additional lyrics*

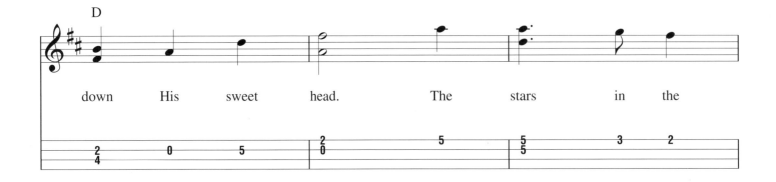

bed, the lit - tle Lord Je - sus laid

down His sweet head. The stars in the

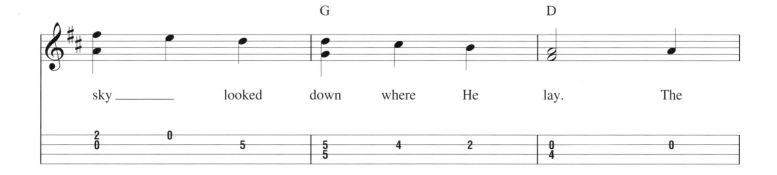

sky _____ looked down where He lay. The

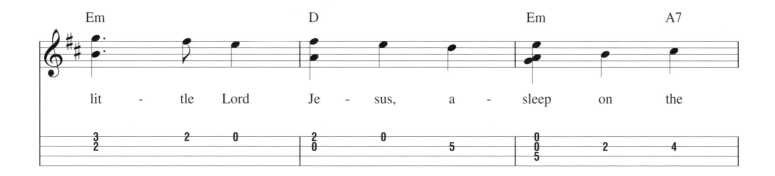

lit - tle Lord Je - sus, a - sleep on the

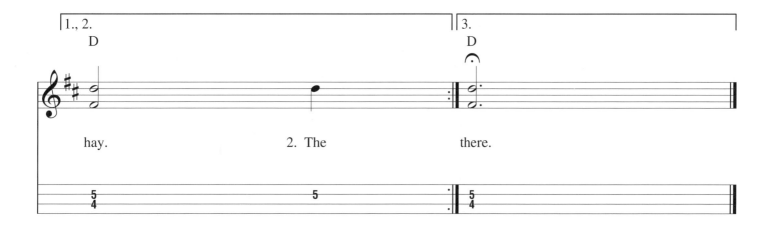

hay. 2. The there.

Additional Lyrics

2. The cattle are lowing, the baby awakes,
   But little Lord Jesus, no crying He makes.
   I love Thee, Lord Jesus, look down from the sky
   And stay by my cradle till morning is nigh.

3. Be near me, Lord Jesus, I ask Thee to stay
   Close by me forever and love me, I pray.
   Bless all the dear children in Thy tender care
   And fit us for heaven to live with Thee there.

Deck the Hall

Traditional Welsh Carol

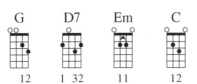

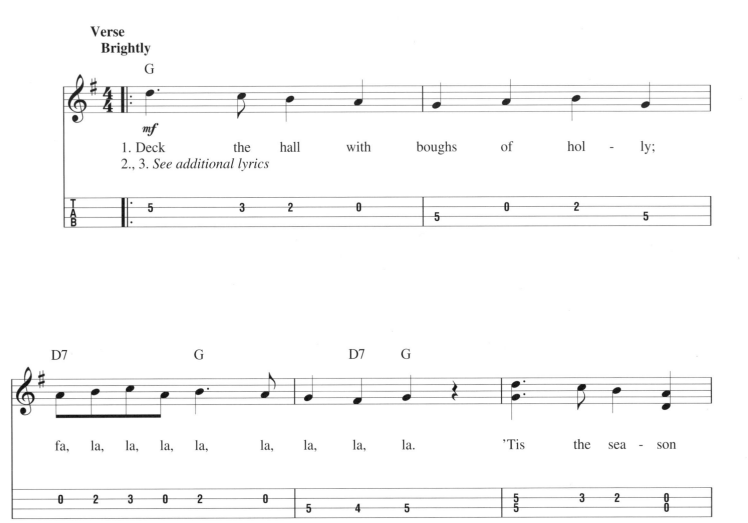

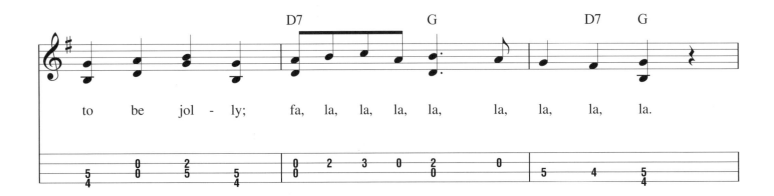

Don we now our gay ap - par - el; fa, la, la, la, la, la,

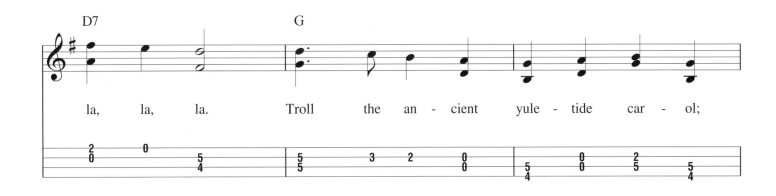

la, la, la. Troll the an - cient yule - tide car - ol;

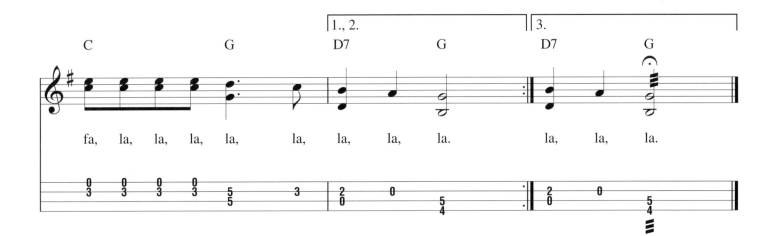

fa, la, la, la, la, la, la, la, la. la, la, la.

Additional Lyrics

2. See the blazing yule before us;
   Fa, la, la, la, la, la, la, la, la.
   Strike the harp and join the chorus;
   Fa, la, la, la, la, la, la, la, la.
   Follow me in merry measure;
   Fa, la, la, la, la, la, la, la, la.
   While I tell of Yuletide treasure;
   Fa, la, la, la, la, la, la, la, la.

3. Fast away the old year passes;
   Fa, la, la, la, la, la, la, la, la.
   Hail the new, ye lads and lasses;
   Fa, la, la, la, la, la, la, la, la.
   Sing we joyous, all together;
   Fa, la, la, la, la, la, la, la, la.
   Heedless of the wind and weather;
   Fa, la, la, la, la, la, la, la, la.

The First Noël

17th Century English Carol
Music from W. Sandy's Christmas Carols

cold win - ter's night _____ that was _____ so

Chorus

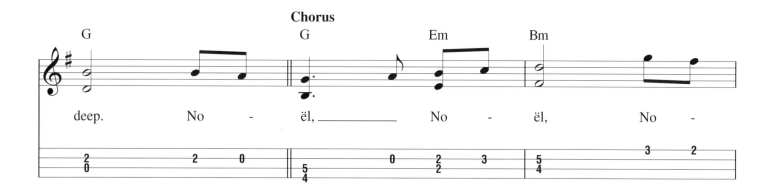

deep. No - ël, _____ No - ël, No -

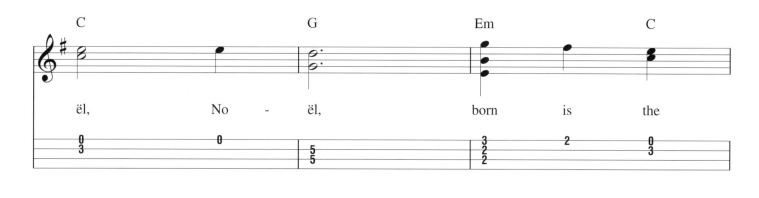

ël, No - ël, born is the

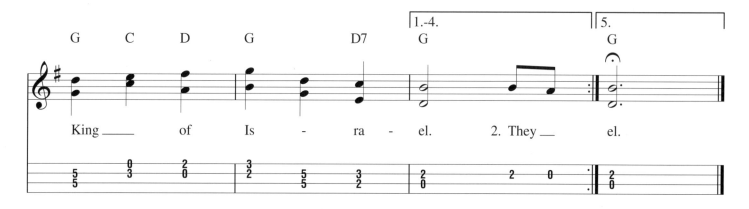

King _____ of Is - ra - el. 2. They ___ el.

Additional Lyrics

2. They looked up and saw a star
   Shining in the east, beyond them far.
   And to the earth it gave great light
   And so it continued both day and night.

3. And by the light of that same star,
   Three wise men came from country far;
   To seek for a King was their intent,
   And to follow the star wherever it went.

4. This star drew nigh to the northwest,
   O'er Bethlehem it took its rest;
   And there it did both stop and stay,
   Right over the place where Jesus lay.

5. Then entered in those wise men three,
   Full reverently upon their knee;
   And offered there in His presence,
   Their gold, and myrrh, and frankincense.

Go, Tell It on the Mountain

African-American Spiritual
Verses by John W. Work, Jr.

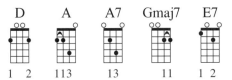

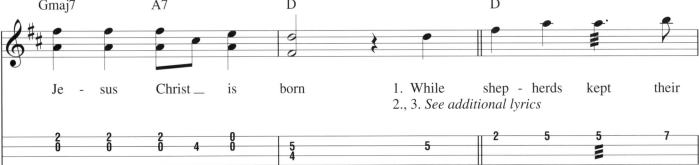

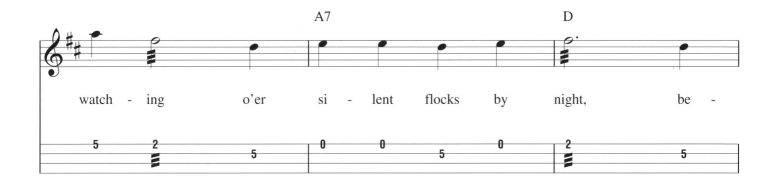

watch - ing   o'er   si - lent   flocks   by   night,   be -

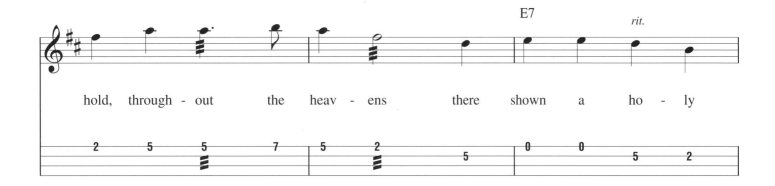

hold,   through - out   the   heav - ens   there   shown   a   ho - ly

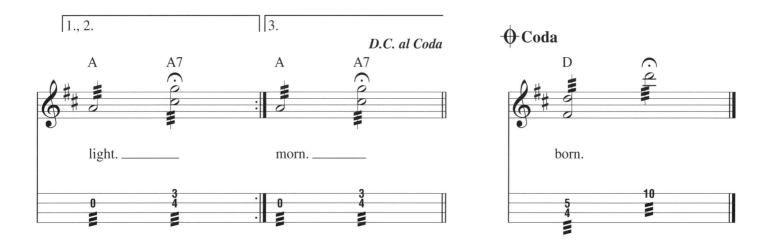

light. _____   morn. _____   born.

Additional Lyrics

2. The shepherds feared and trembled
When, lo! above the earth
Rang out the angel chorus
That hailed our Savior's birth.

3. Down in a lowly manger
Our humble Christ was born.
And God sent us salvation
That blessed Christmas morn.

God Rest Ye Merry, Gentlemen

19th Century English Carol

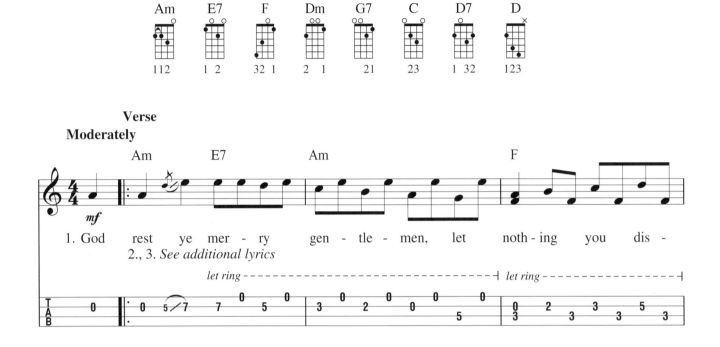

Verse
Moderately

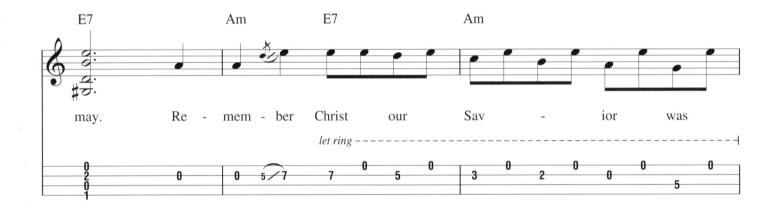

1. God rest ye mer - ry gen - tle - men, let noth - ing you dis -
2., 3. *See additional lyrics*

may. Re - mem - ber Christ our Sav - ior was

born on Christ - mas day to save us all from

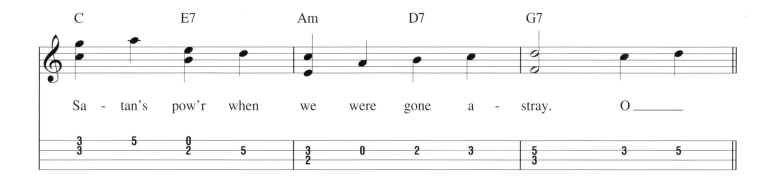

Sa - tan's pow'r when we were gone a - stray. O _____

Chorus

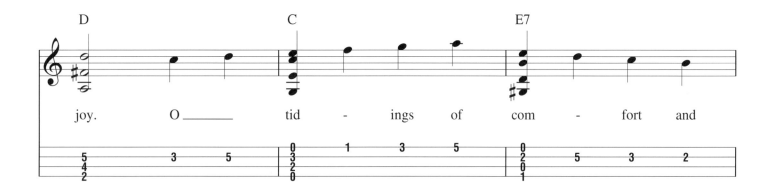

tid - ings of com - fort and joy, com - fort and

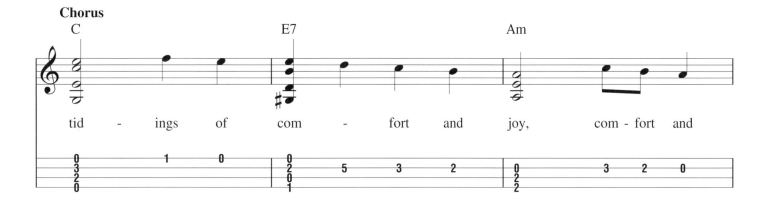

joy. O _____ tid - ings of com - fort and

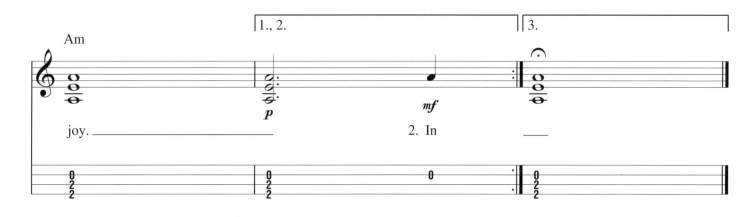

1., 2.

3.

joy. _____ 2. In _____

Additional Lyrics

2. In Bethlehem, in Jewry,
   This blessed babe was born,
   And laid within a manger
   Upon this blessed morn
   That which His mother Mary
   Did nothing take in scorn.

3. From God, our Heav'nly Father,
   A blessed angel came,
   And unto certain shepherds
   Brought tidings of the same.
   How that in Bethlehem was born
   The Son of God by name.

Good King Wenceslas

Words by John M. Neale
Music from Piae Cantiones

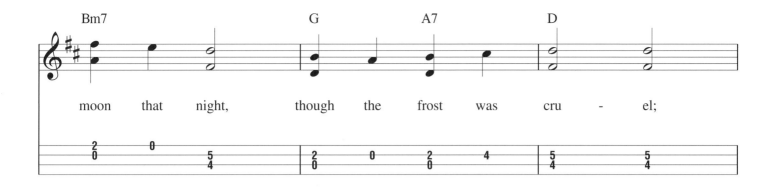

moon that night, though the frost was cru - el;

when a poor man came in sight, gath - 'ring win - ter

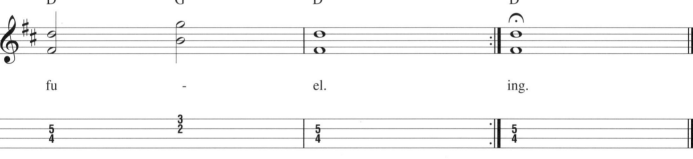

fu - el.

ing.

Additional Lyrics

2. "Hither page, and stand by me,
If thou know'st it telling;
Yonder peasent, who is he?
Where and what his dwelling?"
"Sire, he lives a good league hence,
Underneath the mountain;
Right against the forest fence,
By Saint Agnes fountain."

3. "Bring me flesh, and bring me wine,
Bring me pine-logs hither;
Thou and I will see him dine,
When we bear then thither."
Page and monarch forth they went,
Forth they went together;
Through the rude wind's wild lament,
And the bitter weather.

4. "Sire, the night is darker now,
And the wind blows stronger;
Fails my heart, I know not how,
I can go not longer."
"Mark my footsteps, my good page,
Tread thou in them boldly;
Thou shalt find the winter's rage
Freeze thy blood less coldly."

5. In his master's steps he trod,
Where the snow lay dinted;
Heat was in the very sod
Which the saint has printed.
Therefore, Christmas men, be sure,
Wealth or rank posessing;
Ye who now will bless the poor,
Shall yourselves find blessing.

Hark! The Herald Angels Sing

Words by Charles Wesley
Altered by George Whitefield
Music by Felix Mendelssohn-Bartholdy

Additional Lyrics

2. Christ, by the highest heav'n adored,
   Christ, the everlasting Lord;
   Late in time, behold Him come,
   Offspring of the Virgin's womb.
   Veil'd in flesh, the Godhead see,
   Hail th'Incarnate Deity.
   Pleased as man with man to dwell,
   Jesus, our Emmanuel!
   Hark! The herald angels sing,
   "Glory to the newborn King!"

3. Hail, the heav'n-born Prince of Peace!
   Hail, the Son of Righteousness!
   Light and life to all He brings,
   Ris'n with healing in His wings.
   Mild, He lays His glory by.
   Born, that man no more may die.
   Born to raise the sons of earth,
   Born to give them second birth.
   Hark! The herald angels sing,
   "Glory to the newborn King!"

I Saw Three Ships

Traditional English Carol

Verse
Moderately fast

1. I saw three ships come sail - ing in on
2.-9. *See additional lyrics*

Christ - mas day, _____ on Christ - mas day. I

saw three ships come sail - ing in on

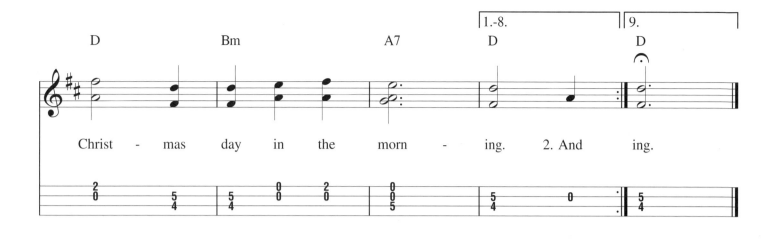

Additional Lyrics

2. And what was in those ships, all three,
   On Christmas day, on Christmas day?
   And what was in those ships, all three,
   On Christmas day in the morning?

3. The Virgin Mary and Christ were there
   On Christmas day, on Christmas day.
   The Virgin Mary and Christ were there
   On Christmas day in the morning.

4. Pray, whither sailed those ships, all three
   On Christmas day, on Christmas day?
   Pray, whither sailed those ships, all three
   On Christmas day in the morning?

5. Oh, they sailed into Bethlehem
   On Christmas day, on Christmas day.
   Oh, they sailed into Bethlehem
   On Christmas day in the morning.

6. And all the bells on earth shall ring
   On Christmas day, on Christmas day.
   And all the bells on earth shall ring
   On Christmas day in the morning.

7. And all the angels in heaven shall sing
   On Christmas day, on Christmas day.
   And all the angels in heaven shall sing
   On Christmas day in the morning.

8. And all the souls on earth shall sing
   On Christmas day, on Christmas day.
   And all the souls on earth shall sing
   On Christmas day in the morning.

9. Then let us all rejoice again
   On Christmas day, on Christmas day.
   Then let us all rejoice again
   On Christmas day in the morning.

It Came Upon the Midnight Clear

Words by Edmund H. Sears
Traditional English Melody
Adapted by Arthur Sullivan

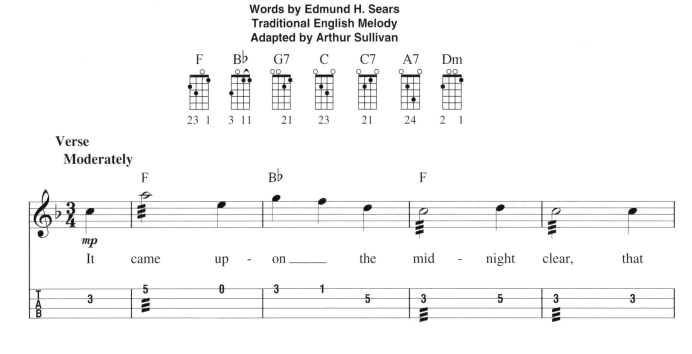

Verse
Moderately

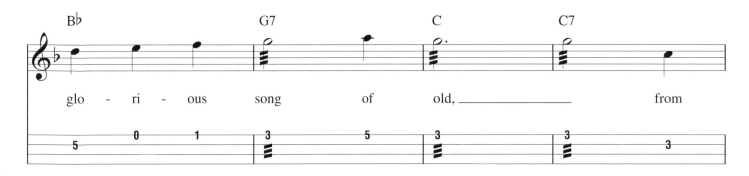

It came up-on _____ the mid-night clear, that

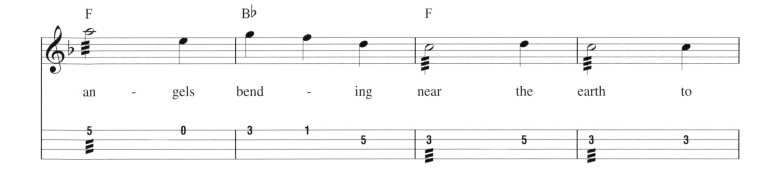

glo-ri-ous song of old, _____ from

an-gels bend-ing near the earth to

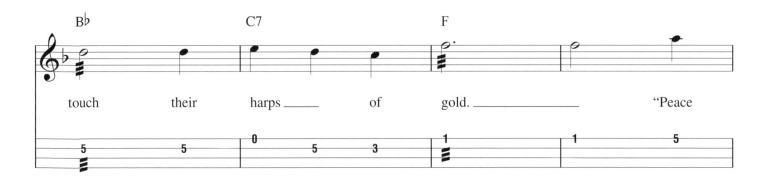

touch their harps ___ of gold. _____ "Peace

on　　　the　　　earth,　　good　　will　　　to　　　men,　　　from

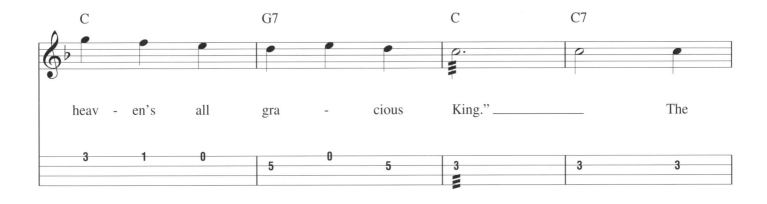

heav - en's　　all　　gra　-　cious　King."　　　　　　The

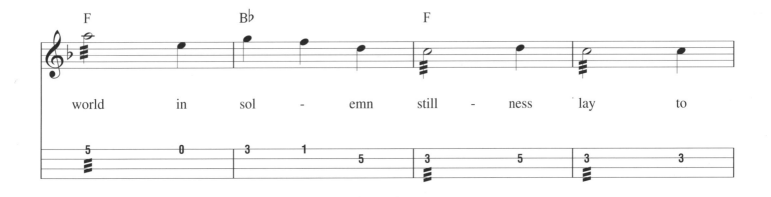

world　　　in　　sol　-　emn　　still　-　ness　　lay　　　to

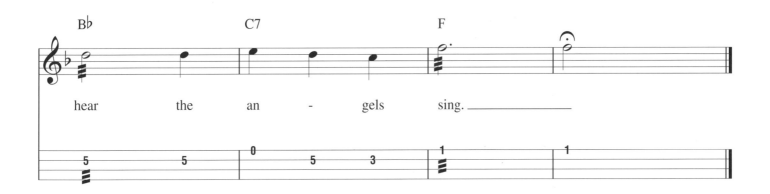

hear　　　the　　an　-　gels　　sing.

Jingle Bells

Words and Music by J. Pierpont

Chorus

Additional Lyrics

2. A day or two ago, I thought I'd take a ride,
   And soon Miss Fannie Bright was sitting by my side.
   The horse was lean and lank,
   Misfortune seemed his lot.
   He got into a drifted bank and we, we got upshot! Oh!

3. Now the ground is white, go it while you're young.
   Take the girls tonight and sing this sleighing song.
   Just get a bobtail bay,
   Two-forty for his speed.
   Then hitch him to an open sleigh and crack, you'll take the lead! Oh!

Joy to the World

Words by Isaac Watts
Music by George Frideric Handel
Arranged by Lowell Mason

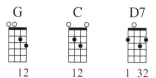

Verse
Moderately fast

1. Joy to the world! The Lord is come. Let
2., 3., 4. See additional lyrics

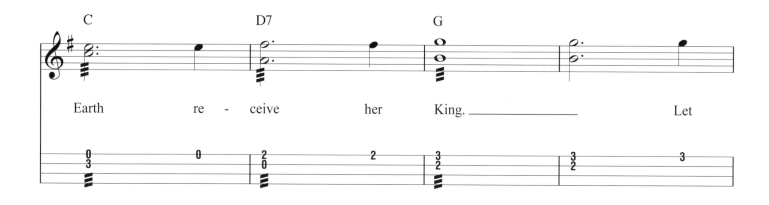

Earth re - ceive her King. _____ Let

ev - 'ry _____ heart _____ pre - pare _____ Him _____

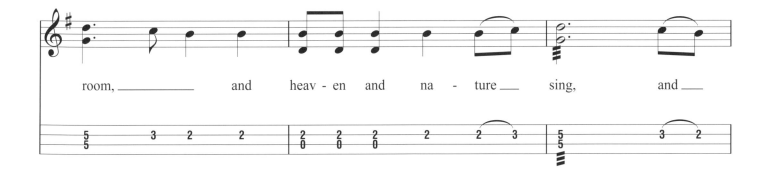

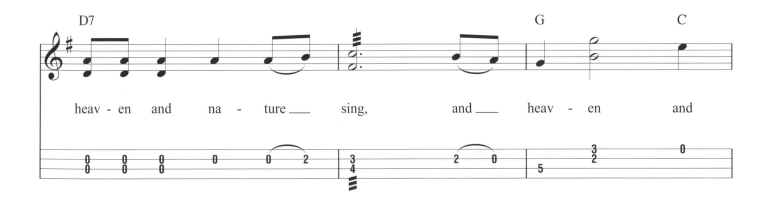

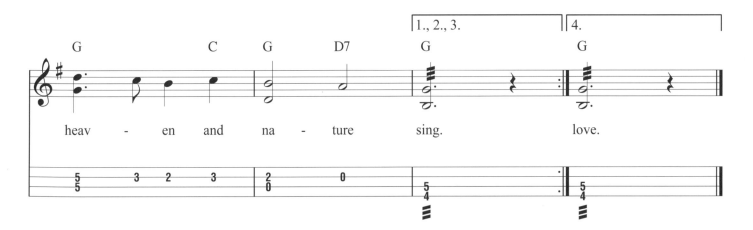

Additional Lyrics

2. Joy to the world! The Savior reigns.
   Let men their songs employ;
   While fields and floods, rocks, hills and plains
   Repeat the sounding joy,
   Repeat the sounding joy,
   Repeat, repeat the sounding joy.

3. No more let sin and sorrow grow,
   Nor thorns infest the ground.
   He comes to make His blessings flow
   Far as the curse is found,
   Far as the curse is found,
   Far as, far as the curse is found.

4. He rules the world with truth and grace,
   And makes the nations prove
   The glories of His righteousness,
   And wonders of His love,
   And wonders of His love,
   And wonders, wonders of His love.

O Christmas Tree

Traditional German Carol

Verse

Moderately

1. O Christ-mas tree! O Christ-mas tree,____ you stand in ver-dant
2., 3. *See additional lyrics*

beau - ty! O Christ - mas tree, O Christ - mas tree,_____ you

stand in ver-dant beau-ty!_____ Your boughs are green____ in

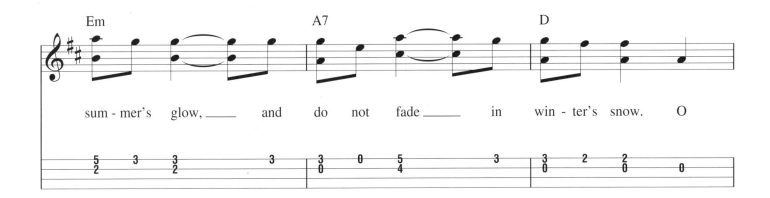

sum - mer's glow, _____ and do not fade _____ in win - ter's snow. O

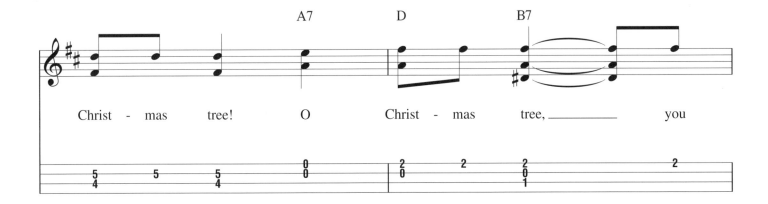

Christ - mas tree! O Christ - mas tree, _____ you

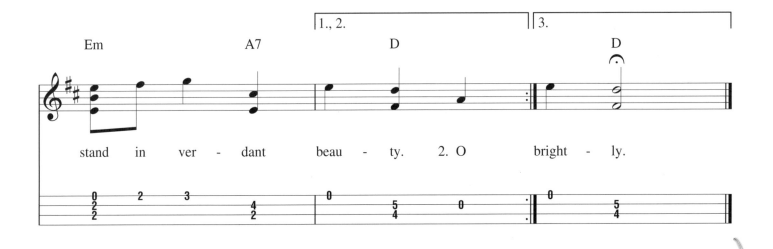

stand in ver - dant beau - ty. 2. O bright - ly.

Additional Lyrics

2. O Christmas tree! O Christmas tree,
   Much pleasure doth thou bring me!
   O Christmas tree! O Christmas tree,
   Much pleasure doth thou bring me!
   For every year the Christmas tree
   Brings to us all both joy and glee.
   O Christmas tree! O Christmas tree,
   Much pleasure doth thou bring me!

3. O Christmas tree! O Christmas tree,
   Thy candles shine out brightly!
   O Christmas tree! O Christmas tree,
   Thy candles shine out brightly!
   Each bough doth hold its tiny light
   That makes each toy to sparkle bright.
   O Christmas tree! O Christmas tree,
   Thy candles shine out brightly.

O Come, All Ye Faithful
(Adeste Fideles)

Words and Music by John Francis Wade
Latin Words translated by Frederick Oakeley

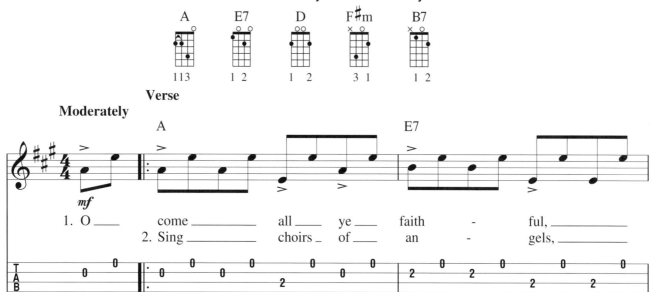

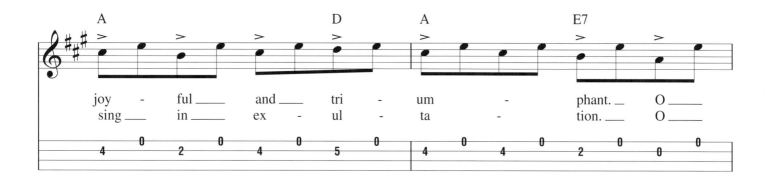

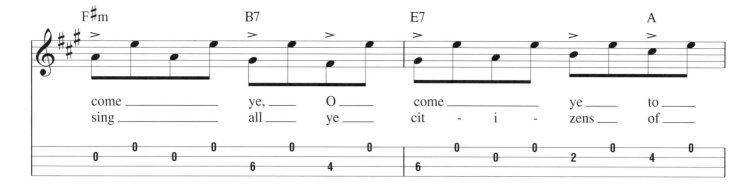

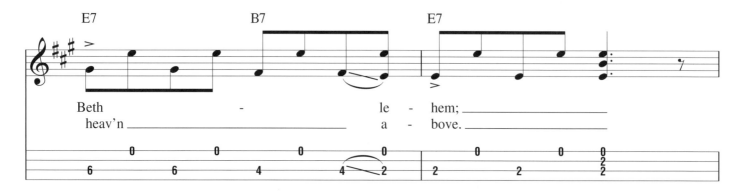

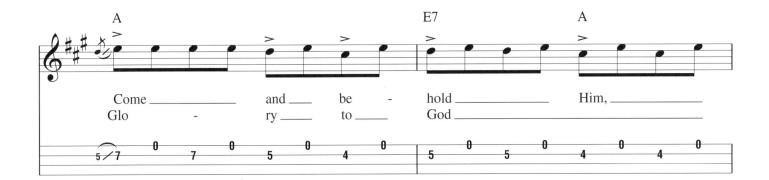

Come _____ and ___ be - hold _____ Him, _____
Glo - ry ___ to ___ God _____

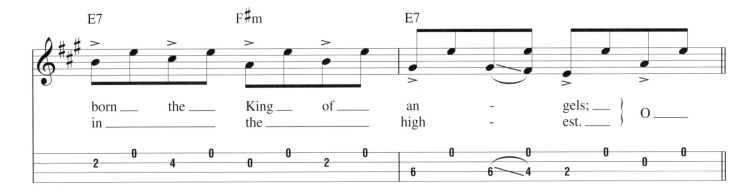

born ___ the ___ King ___ of ___ an - gels; ___ } O ___
in _____ the _____ high - est. ___

Chorus

come, _ let _ us _ a - dore _____ Him. _ O ___ come, _ let _ us _ a -

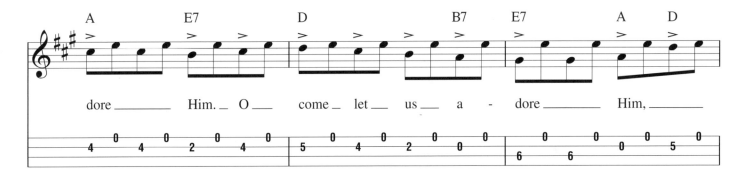

dore _____ Him. _ O ___ come _ let _ us ___ a - dore _____ Him, ___

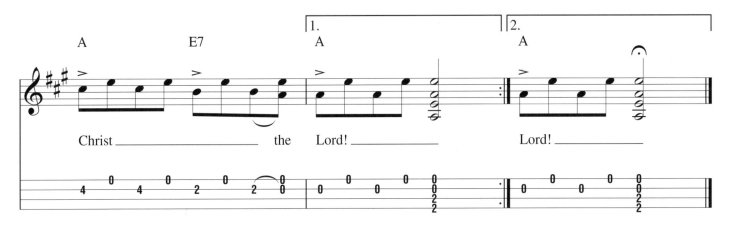

1.
2.

Christ _____ the Lord! _____ Lord! _____

O Come, O Come, Emmanuel

Traditional Latin Text
V. 1,2 translated by John M. Neale
V. 3,4 translated by Henry S. Coffin
15th Century French Melody
Adapted by Thomas Helmore

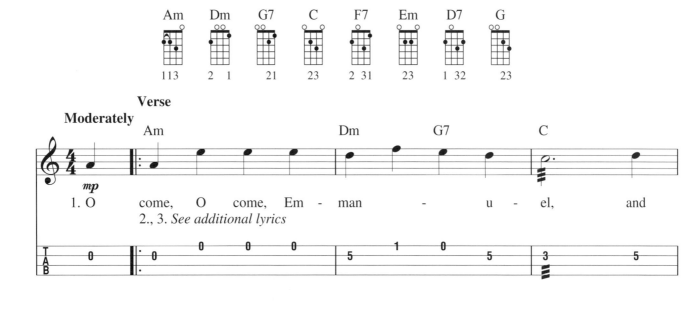

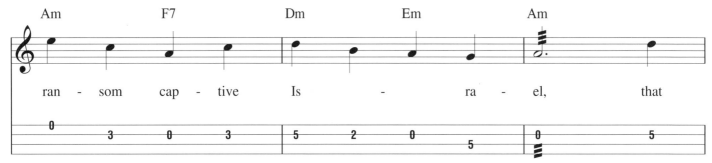

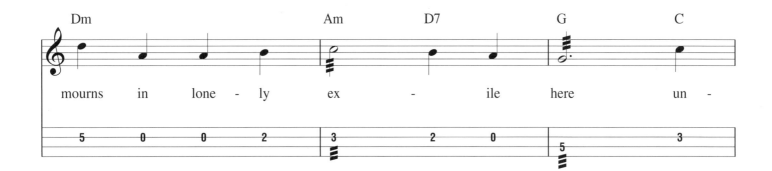

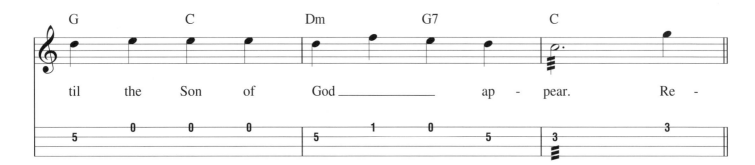

Chorus

joice,   re - joice!   Em - man - u -

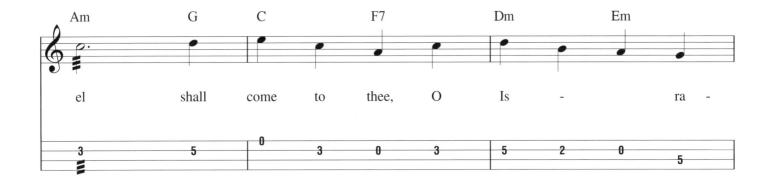

el   shall   come   to   thee,   O   Is - ra -

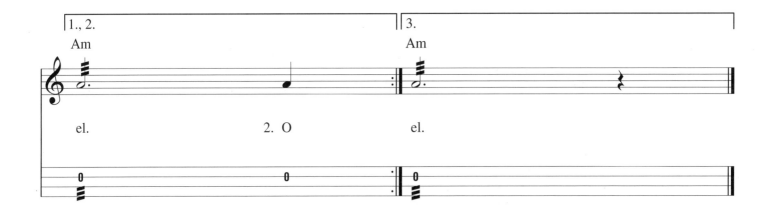

el.   2. O   el.

Additional Lyrics

2. O come, Thou Wisdom from on high,
   And order all things far and nigh;
   To us, the path of knowledge show
   And cause us in her ways to go.

3. O come, Desire of nations, bind
   All people in one heart and mind;
   Bid envy, strife, and quarrels cease;
   Fill the whole world with heaven's peace.

O Holy Night

French Words by Placide Cappeau
English Words by John S. Dwight
Music by Adolphe Adam

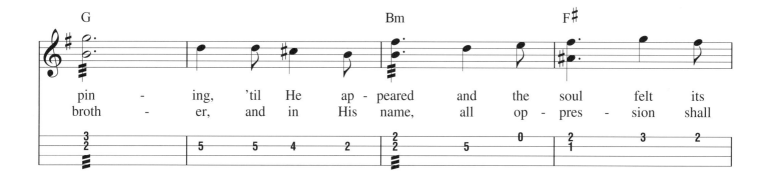

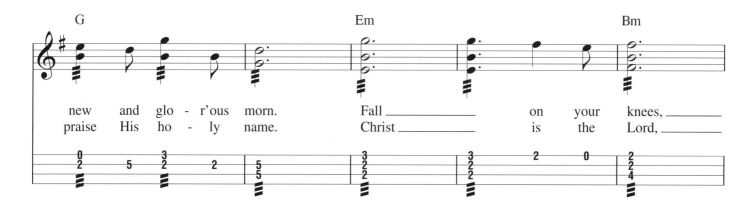

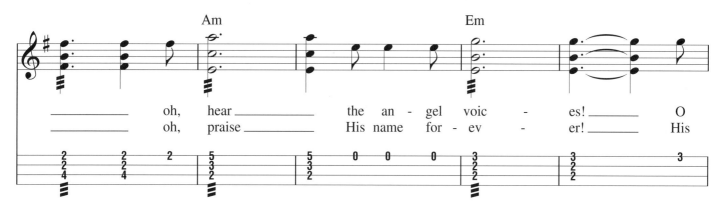

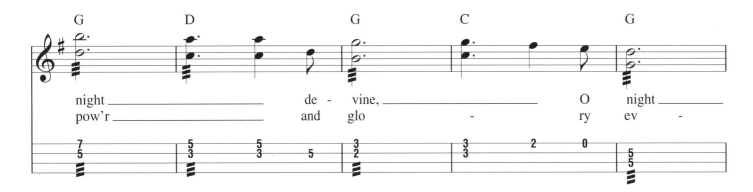

night _____ de - vine, _____ O night _____
pow'r _____ and glo - ry ev -

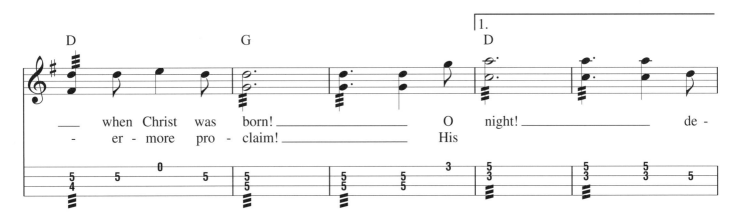

___ when Christ was born! _____ O night! _____ de -
- er - more pro - claim! _____ His

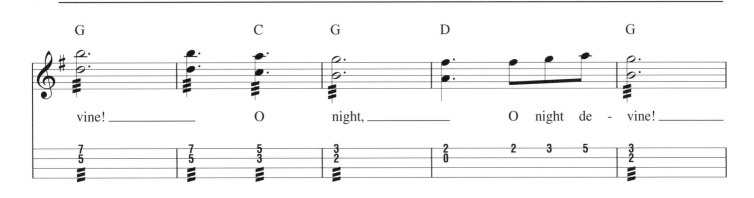

vine! _____ O night, _____ O night de - vine! _____

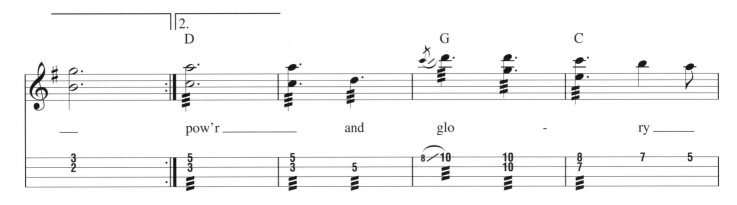

___ pow'r _____ and glo - ry _____

ev - er - more pro - claim. _____

Jolly Old St. Nicholas

Traditional 19th Century American Carol

Verse
Moderately fast

mf

1. Jol - ly old Saint Nich - o - las, lean your ear this way. _____
2., 3. *See additional lyrics*

Don't you tell a sin - gle soul what I'm going to say. _____

Christ - mas Eve is com - ing soon, now, you dear old man, _____

whis - per what you'll bring to me; tell me if you can. _____ best. _____

Additional Lyrics

2. When the clock is striking twelve, when I'm fast asleep,
   Down the chimney broad and black, with your pack you'll creep.
   All the stockings you will find hanging in a row.
   Mine will be the shortest one, you'll be sure to know.

3. Johnny wants a pair of skates; Suzy wants a sled.
   Nellie wants a picture book, yellow, blue and red.
   Now I think I'll leave to you what to give the rest.
   Choose for me, dear Santa Claus, you will know the best.

O Little Town of Bethlehem

Words by Phillips Brooks
Music by Lewis H. Redner

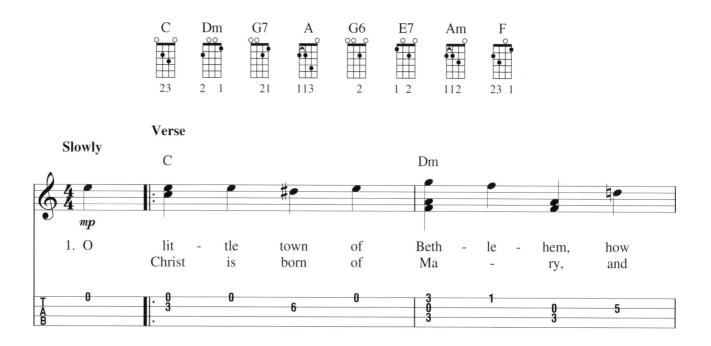

Verse

Slowly

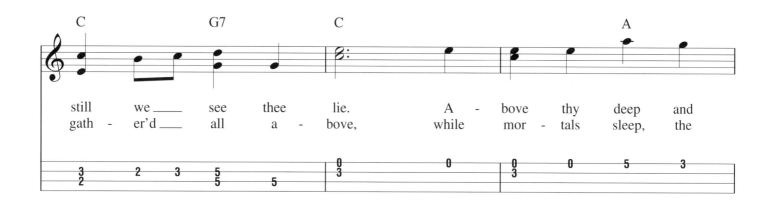

1. O lit - tle town of Beth - le - hem, how
   Christ is born of Ma - ry, and

still we ___ see thee lie. A - bove thy deep and
gath - er'd ___ all a - bove, while mor - tals sleep, the

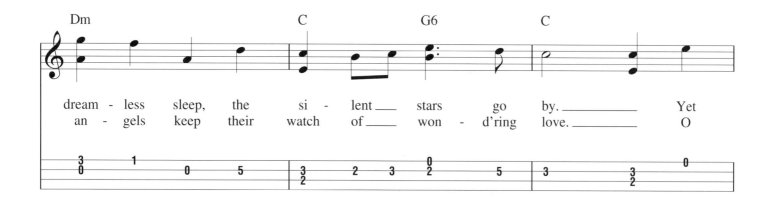

dream - less sleep, the si - lent ___ stars go by. ___ Yet
an - gels keep their watch of ___ won - d'ring love. ___ O

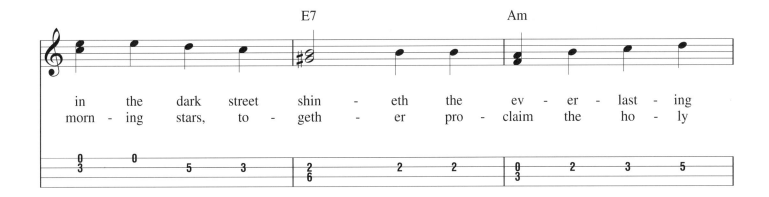

in the dark street shin - eth the ev - er - last - ing
morn - ing stars, to - geth - er pro - claim the ho - ly

light; the hopes and fears of all the years are
birth! And prais - es sing to God the King, and

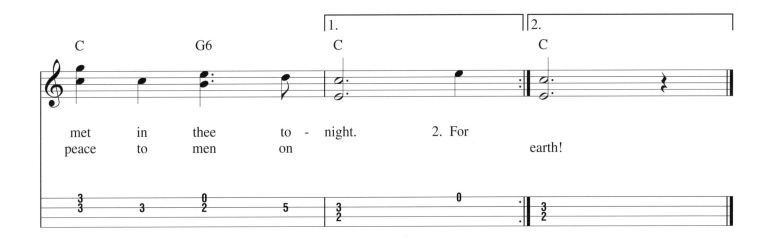

met in thee to - night.   2. For
peace to men on   earth!

Silent Night

Words by Joseph Mohr
Translated by John F. Young
Music by Franz X. Gruber

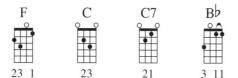

Verse
Moderately slow

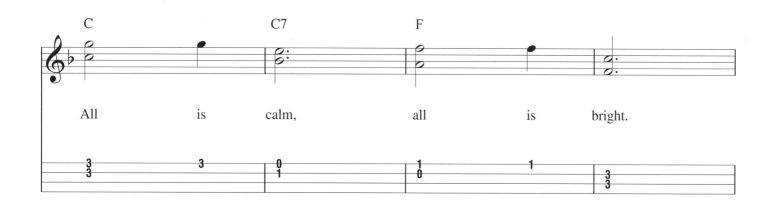

1. Si - lent night, ho - ly night!
2., 3. *See additional lyrics*

All is calm, all is bright.

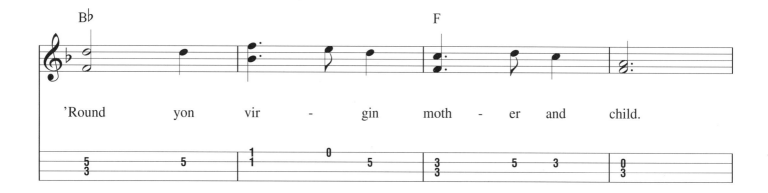

'Round yon vir - gin moth - er and child.

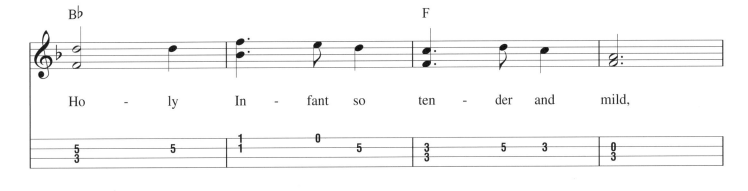

Ho - ly In - fant so ten - der and mild,

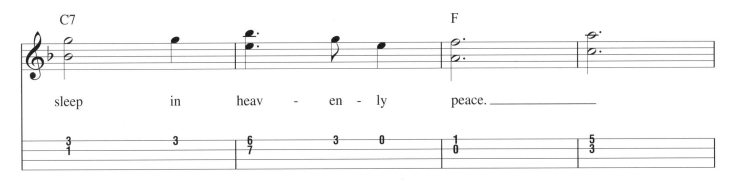

sleep in heav - en - ly peace. _____

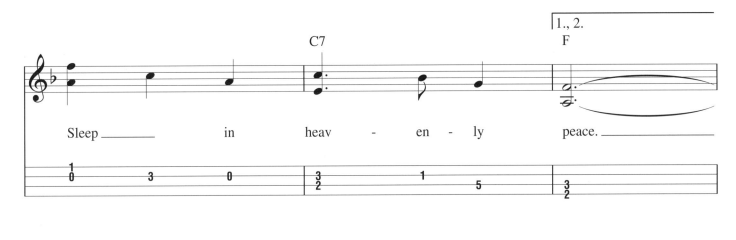

1., 2.

Sleep ____ in heav - en - ly peace. _____

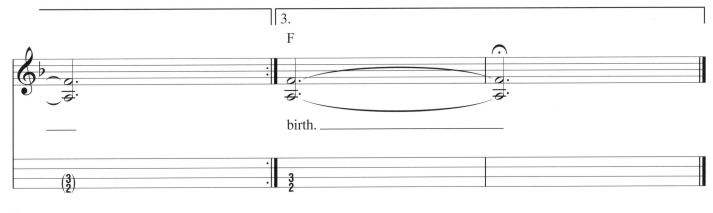

3.

____ birth. _____

Additional Lyrics

2. Silent night, holy night!
Shepherds quake at the sight.
Glories stream from heaven afar.
Heavenly hosts sing Alleluia.
Christ the Savior is born!
Christ the Savior is born!

3. Silent night, holy night!
Son of God, love's pure light.
Radiant beams from Thy holy face
With the dawn of redeeming grace,
Jesus, Lord at Thy birth.
Jesus, Lord at Thy birth.

Up on the Housetop

Words and Music by B.R. Handy

Chorus

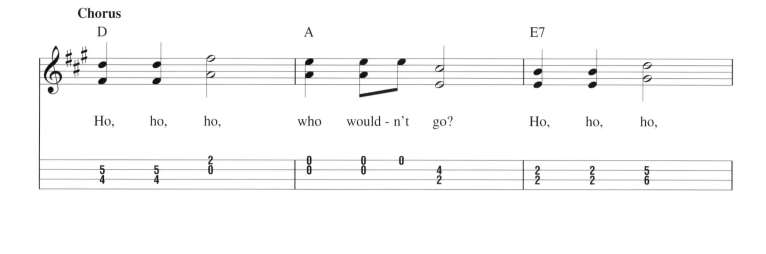

Ho, ho, ho, who would-n't go? Ho, ho, ho,

who would-n't go? _____ Up on the house - top, click, click, click.

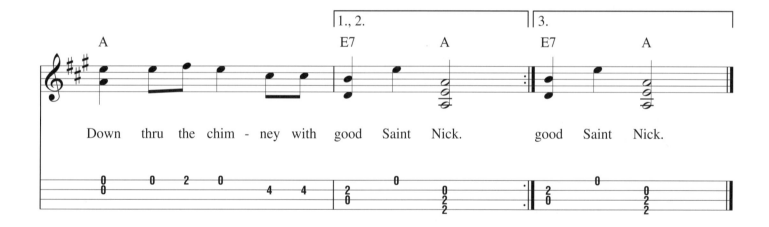

Down thru the chim - ney with good Saint Nick.   good Saint Nick.

Additional Lyrics

2. First comes the stocking of little Nell,
Oh, dear Santa, fill it well.
Give her a dollie that laughs and cries,
One that will open and shut her eyes.

3. Next comes the stocking of little Will,
Oh, just see what a glorious fill!
Here is a hammer and lots of tacks,
Also a ball and a whip that cracks.

We Wish You a Merry Christmas

Traditional English Folksong

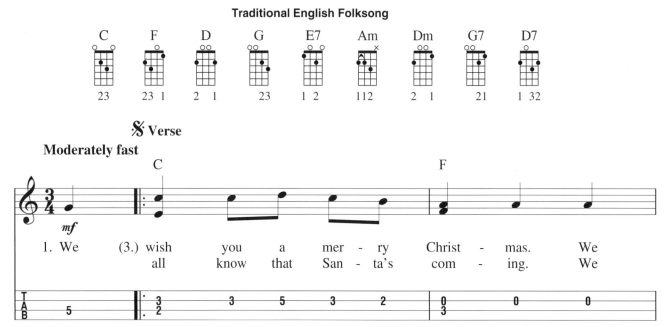

% Verse

Moderately fast

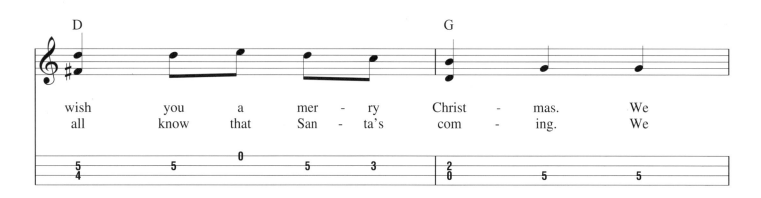

1. We (3.) wish you a mer - ry Christ - mas. We
   all know that San - ta's com - ing. We

wish you a mer - ry Christ - mas. We
all know that San - ta's com - ing. We

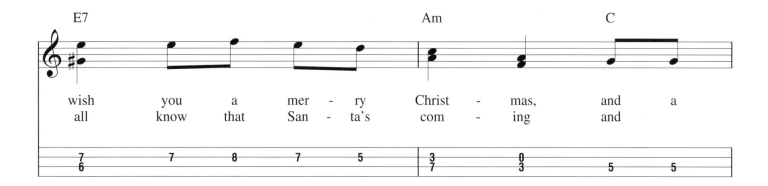

wish you a mer - ry Christ - mas, and a
all know that San - ta's com - ing and

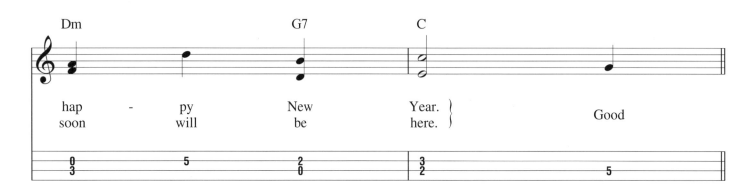

hap - py New Year. } Good
soon will be here. }

What Child Is This?

Words by William C. Dix
16th Century English Melody

Additional Lyrics

2. Why lies He in such mean estate
Where ox and ass are feeding?
Good Christian, fear, for sinners here
The silent word is pleading.

3. So bring Him incense, gold and myrrh.
Come, peasant King, to own Him.
The King of Kings salvation brings,
Let loving hearts enthrone Him.

We Three Kings of Orient Are

Words and Music by John H. Hopkins, Jr.

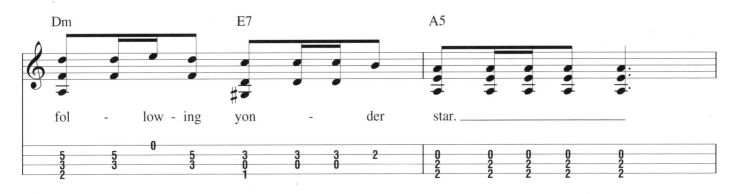

fol - low - ing yon - der star. _____

Chorus

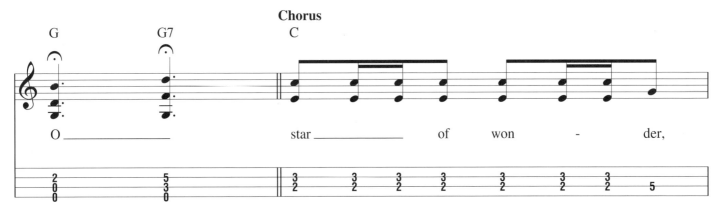

O _____ star _____ of won - der,

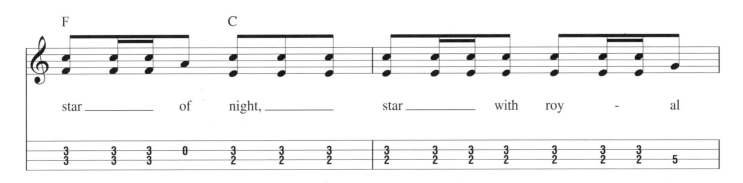

star _____ of night, _____ star _____ with roy - al

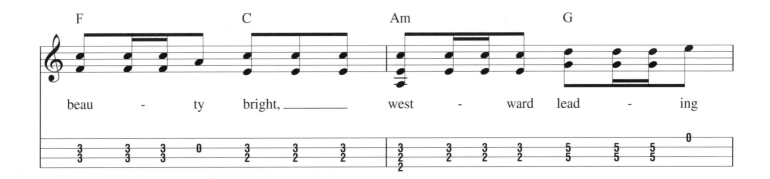

beau - ty bright, _____ west - ward lead - ing

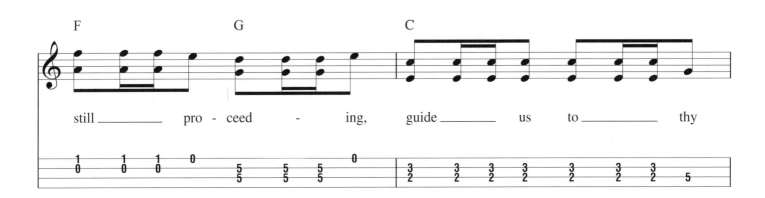

still _____ pro - ceed - ing, guide _____ us to _____ thy

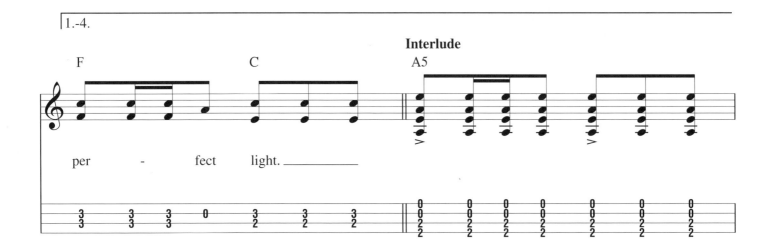

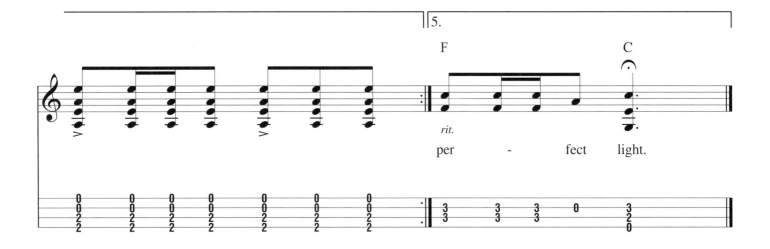

Additional Lyrics

2. Born a King on Bethlehem plain,
   Gold I bring to crown him again.
   King forever, ceasing never,
   Over us all to reign.

3. Frankincense to offer have I;
   Incense owns a Deity nigh;
   Prayer and praising, all men raising,
   Worship Him, God most high.

4. Myrrh is mine: it's bitter perfume
   Breathes a life of gathering gloom:
   Sorrowing, sighing, bleeding, dying;
   Sealed in the stone-cold tomb.

5. Glorious now, behold Him arise,
   King and God, and Sacrifice!
   Heav'n sings alleluia,
   Alleluia the earth replies: